W9-AMN-787

J

Eri

What
Is
God
Like ?

Mary E. Erickson

Illustrated by
Anita C. Nelson

ChariotVICTOR
PUBLISHING
A Division of Cook Communications

Chariot Books is an imprint of ChariotVictor Publishing,
a division of Cook Communications, Colorado Springs, Colorado 80918
Cook Communications, Paris, Ontario
Kingsway Communications, Eastbourne, England

WHAT IS GOD LIKE?

Unless otherwise indicated, all Scripture quotations in this publication are from the *Holy
Bible, New International Version*. Copyright © 1973, 1978, 1984, International Bible Society.

Designed by Donna Nelson

First printing, 1990
Printed in Singapore
99 98 97 96   8 7 6

LIBRARY OF CONGRESS
Library of Congress Cataloging-in-Publication Data

Erickson, Mary E.
    What is God like? / by Mary E. Erickson; illustrated byAnita Nelson.
        p.   cm.
    Summary: Uses Bible verses describing God to explain his many attributes and
how he cares for us.
    ISBN 1-55513-273-1
    1. God--Juvenile literature. [1. God.] I. Nelson, Anita C.,
1949- ill. II. Title.
BT107.E75   1990
231--dc20   89-39729
                                                   CIP
                                                   AC

Dedicated to
Kaleb Tabben,
my four-year-old
grandson,
still soft clay being
molded into a choice
vessel for use in
God's kingdom
M.E.E.

Dedicated to
Mark A. Nelson,
my best friend
and husband
A.C.N.

Have you ever heard someone say, "I'm as hungry as a bear," or "You eat like a pig!" or "It's as soft as a bunny"?

People often describe things they see, feel, smell, hear, or taste by comparing them to other things. Sometimes we call each other names of animals or things like *sunshine, monkey*, or *sugar-plum*. If your mom calls you *sunshine*, she means you're a happy person who brings cheer to others. If your grandpa calls you a *monkey*, he means you're a funny person who makes others laugh!

In the Bible there are many comparisons like these to help us understand what God is like. We will talk about some of these comparisons in this book. They will help you understand a little better what God is like—and how much He loves and cares for you.

God is like a **Potter**

Yet, O Lord, you are our Father. We are the clay, you are the potter; we are all the work of your hand.
Isaiah 64:8

A potter is someone who shapes things out of clay.

First he chooses a lump of soft clay. "What shall I make?" he asks himself. "A plain soup bowl? a strong water jug? a fancy flower vase?"

He puts the wet clay on the potter's wheel. With firm fingers he presses and pushes and shapes the clay into whatever he wants to make.

When the vessel is done, the potter smiles. "There's not another one like it!" he says. He likes each one, whether it's an everyday dish or a beautiful vase.

There's no one else exactly like me. Like a potter shaping a vessel, God made me just the way He wanted me to be.

God is like the **Rain**

He will come to us like the winter rains, like the spring rains that water the earth.
Hosea 6:3

You know what rain is—drops of water that fall from the clouds.

Rain waters the grass and gardens. It makes plants and trees grow, so they can make fruits and vegetables.

Rain fills the streams and rivers where fish live and animals drink.

Rain gives us water for drinking, cooking, and bathing. Plants, animals, and people all need the rain.

Just as the rain brings life to all nature, God brings life to me.

God is like a Shepherd

He tends his flock like a shepherd: He gathers the lambs in his arms and carries them close to his heart.
Isaiah 40:11

A shepherd is the person who takes care of a flock of sheep.

Each day the shepherd leads his sheep beside shallow streams of water and lets them eat grass in the meadows.

The shepherd must be brave. He has to protect his sheep in stormy weather, on rocky cliffs, and from wild wolves.

At night the shepherd counts his sheep and guards them while they sleep. He knows each one by name.

God loves and cares for me just like a good shepherd takes care of his sheep.

God is like a **Refuge**

The Lord is
good, a refuge
in times of
trouble.
He cares for
those who
trust in him.
Nahum 1:7

A refuge is a place safe from danger or trouble. It's a good place to go for protection or shelter.

People cut down trees and dig up meadows in order to build houses, towns, and factories. When this happens, many birds and animals lose their homes.

Sometimes a person will say, "These animals will die unless we help them. Let's fence in some land and make some laws so no one can build or trap or fish or hunt there."

A place like this is called a "wildlife refuge." Birds, fish, and animals who live there are protected from danger. They can find food, build a nest or den, and raise their babies safely.

God is like a refuge to me. I can count on Him to help me when I am in trouble and to protect me from danger.

God is like a **Rock**

O Lord . . . be my rock of refuge, to which I can always go.
Psalm 71:1, 3

A rock is a huge mass of stone. Some rocks are so big and strong, they cannot be moved. Have you ever seen a rock that big?

A rock can be a resting place on a dusty hiking trail.

A rock can be a safe place to get away from wind or rain.

A rock can be a hiding place when enemies are near.

Whenever I need help, I will trust in God, because He is strong and immovable as a rock.

God is like a Guide

For this God is our God for ever and ever; he will be our guide even to the end.
Psalm 48:14

A guide is someone who leads the way. He knows what to watch out for and which path is best to take.

Indian scouts used to guide explorers through rugged mountain passes. They knew where to find cool water and places to rest.

When a forest ranger takes campers up the hiking trail, he tells them about the trees, ferns, and flowers. "Don't touch that poison ivy," he warns.

A sea pilot knows where rocks and sand lie hidden in the harbor. On stormy days or moonless nights, he guides the ship safely into shore.

God wants to be my guide and choose the best path for me. I need to be a good follower.

God is like a **Pine Tree**

I am like a
green pine
tree; your
fruitfulness
comes from
me.

Hosea 14:8

A pine tree has woody brown cones and leaves like green needles.

Many trees lose their leaves every winter and look like they are dead—but not the pine tree! In summer rain or winter snow, the pine tree stays the same. Its needles are always green, and its branches are always strong.

Any time of year, birds called "pine siskins" find food and shelter in pine trees. They build nests from twigs and bark, and they eat the seeds from the brown pine cones.

God is like a pine tree—living and strong. He supplies what I need all year long.

God is like a King

For the Lord,
the God above
all gods,
is awesome
beyond words;
he is the great
King of all the
earth.
Psalm 47:2
(TLB)

A king is the leader of his land. He has great power—and a big job. He is in charge of directing the country and protecting its people.

A wise king makes good laws so his people can live safely and happily.

Sometimes a king wears a crown and a royal purple robe.   He sits upon a beautiful throne, and all the people of his kingdom honor and respect him.

God is the king above all kings, so I will honor and obey Him..

God is like a Lamp

You are my lamp, O Lord; the Lord turns my darkness into light.
II Samuel 22:29

    A lamp gives off light so you can see in the darkness.

    When you turn on a flashlight, your path becomes plain. Even on a starless night, you won't stumble or fall.

    When you turn on the lamp by your bed, the darkness disappears. You're cozy and comfortable . . . and soon fast asleep.

God is like a lamp to me. He makes my pathway clear and bright. He chases away my fear of night.

God is like a Gardener

God said, "I . . . planted you like a choice vine of sound and reliable stock."
Jeremiah 2:21

A gardener is the person who plants a garden and takes care of it. First the gardener chooses the very best spot. Then he removes the rocks. With heavy tools, he digs up the earth and rakes the soil smooth.

To keep animals out, he builds a sturdy fence. Then he plants the seeds. Each day he hoes the rows, pulls out the weeds, and gives his plants a drink.

To make the vines strong, he cuts off dead branches. With a happy heart, he watches his garden grow.

Someday he'll invite his friends to share the garden's delicious fruit.

I am like a vine in God's garden. He'll help me grow into a person who will do good things for Him.

God is like a Judge

The Lord
takes his place
in court;
he rises to
judge the
people.
Isaiah 3:13

A judge is an officer of the government. He decides if people are innocent or guilty of breaking laws.

A judge sits behind a tall desk. People who have been accused of breaking laws tell him their stories.

He listens carefully and patiently so he can judge who is right and who is wrong. He must be wise and fair.

After he hears all the facts, he decides if people are innocent or not. He has power to punish people who have done wrong.

Someday God will judge all people. Because Jesus died for my sins, and I trust Him as my Savior, I know God has forgiven me.

God is like an **Eagle**

He spreads his wings over them, even as an eagle overspreads her young. She carries them upon her wings— as does the Lord his people!
Deuteronomy 32:11 (TLB)

Have you ever seen an eagle? It is one of the largest birds in the world.

The eagle stretches her wings out over her nest and protects her babies from harm.

She captures small animals and feeds them to her eaglets until they are old enough to catch their own food.

Sometimes an eaglet gets tired while flying. Then the mother eagle swoops down beneath the baby and carries it safely home on her strong wings.

Just as an eagle protects its young ones, God will protect me.

God is like the **Sun**

For the Lord
God is a sun
and shield;
the Lord
bestows favor
and honor.
Psalm 84:11

The sun is the biggest and brightest star in the sky. It's the center of our solar system.

The sun gives us light so we can read and work and play. If the sun did not shine, the earth would always be as black as night.

The sun gives us heat so we are comfortable and warm. If the sun did not shine, our world would be as cold as ice.

The sun gives energy so plants, animals, and people can grow. If the sun did not shine, all living things would die.

God is as important as the sun to me. He brings me life and happiness and makes me feel warm and loving in my heart.

God is like an **Architect**

For Abraham
was looking
forward to the
city with
foundations,
whose
architect
and builder
is God.
Hebrews 11:10

An architect designs and draws plans for big buildings. He gives the builders directions for their work.

God was the architect for the beautiful temple in Jerusalem. He put the plans into King David's mind, and King Solomon, David's son, built the temple.

In a poem, King David wrote that God was the architect of his life, too, because God planned each day of his life before he was born.

God is the architect for my life, too. I'll follow His directions so I can become what God wants me to be.